—

A BRIEF HISTORY OF JAMES BALLENTINE & VFW POST 246

—

Written by Nicholas Garbis
Design & Layout by Craig Rittler
Minneapolis, MN, USA
© November 2019

ISBN: 978-0-578-59796-6 (Paperback)

Book design by Craig Rittler.

Printed by Bookmobile in Minneapolis, Minnesota, United States of America.

First printing edition 2019.

Correspondence to the author and designer can be sent to the Uptown VFW. 2916 Lyndale Ave S. Minneapolis, MN 55408.

Dedicated to the members of
the Veterans of Foreign Wars
Ballentine Post 246,
current, past, and future.

- - -

Lieutenant James Jerome Ballentine
was killed in action on the 9th of
October in 1918, near Madeleine Farm
just south of Cunel, a small town in
eastern France.

On that day, in the final weeks of the
Great War, during the Meuse-Argonne
Offensive, Ballentine's platoon was
advancing against the German line
south of Cunel. Just after taking a
small hill called Bois de Cunel under
heavy fire, a fellow officer was hit by
shrapnel from a shell that exploded
nearby. Ballentine paused to provide
a quick bandage, then left to rejoin

his platoon. He never made it back
to them. Though it is not certain,
we can presume that James Ballentine
died while running across the cratered
earth, running to the front line.

James Ballentine died on his first
day in battle. He was 25 years old.

The war ended 32 days later.

James was buried in a temporary
cemetery at Madeleine Farm, then
moved later to the Meuse-Argonne
American Cemetery at Romagne. In
1921, his family had his body
disinterred and returned home to
Minneapolis, where he was reburied
with full military rites on
September 17, 1921, on a small hill
in Lakewood Cemetery.

The memory of James Ballentine is
honored each year on Memorial Day
by the Veterans of Foreign Wars Post
246 which bears his name.

- - -

CHAPTER 1: Champion

- - -

James Jerome Ballentine was born July
25, 1893, in Rochester, Minnesota
to Helen and Stuart Ballentine. The
Ballentine's had two more sons, Fred
in 1898, and John in 1900, followed
by twin daughters, Mary and Helen in
1909. At the time of the Great War,
the family lived at 3613 Harriet
Avenue South in Minneapolis. Stuart
was a partner in Currier & Ballentine
Printers located at 7th and Hennepin
downtown, and James and his brothers
would also work in the printing
business.

James, or as his firends called him,

"Jimmie", attended South High School
from 1908 until he graduated in 1912.
He played on the South High football
team that won the city-wide champion-
ship and he was Vice President of his
class, but his brightest moments were
on the track. In his senior year, he
dominated the quarter mile sprint,
winning that event at every meet he
entered including a record-breaking
victory at the prestigious Stagg
Interscholastic Track Meet held at
the University of Chicago. Against a
field of 67 competitors, he ran the
440 yard dash in 52.25 seconds.

South High School Yearbook, 1912-13

After graduating from South High, James continued his academic and athletic pursuits at Hamline University. He played football, with notable speed and a new nickname of "Cutesy", a reference to his small stature. He proved himself a champion once again. In 1914, James set a new Tri State record in the 100-yard dash at 10.0 seconds and was a member of Hamline's 4x200 relay team that won at the Drake Relays in Des Moines.

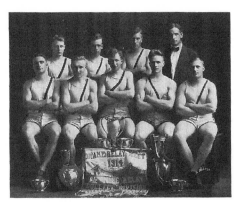

Hamline University: 1914 Track Team

In the fall of 1914, James transferred
to the University of Minnesota and
joined the football and track teams.

"Speedy, but
usually late."
Universtity of
Minnesota Yearbook,
1916

In the two years before the United
States entered the Great War, the Golden
Gophers football team was among the best
in the school's history. The 1915 team
won the Western Conference (which
became the Big Ten in the 1917 season).
They were stopped just short of
perfection: six wins, no losses,
and one tie.

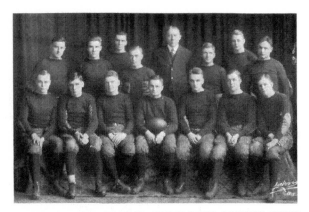

SPRAFKA WYMAN LONG JOHNSON DR. WILLIAMS HANSEN BALLENTINE TENHOFF
QUIST HAUSER DUNNIGAN BIERMAN (Capt.) SINCLAIR TURNQUIST BASTON

FOOT BALL IN 1915

The following season, in 1916, the
Gophers dominated their rivals,
holding them scoreless in most games
and putting up 348 points to their
opponents' 28.

The 1916 Gopher track team also en-
joyed many successes, despite being
a team light on experience. James
continued his strong performances in
the 100 and 220 yard dashes and in

the relays. At the end of the season
he was elected captain for the 1917
team. By the next season, however,
James would be a soldier, and on his
way to France.

Ballentine, on the right, winning a dash.

The sports pages of the day were dense
with short pieces covering high school
and college sports. Through his athletic achievements, James appeared
often in the sports section of the The
Minneapolis Morning Tribune. One short
piece even highlighted a detail as
minor as his 1913 ankle injury, and
the disastrous impact it would have
on the Hamline track team.

When the United States officially
entered the Great War in April of
1917, most of the local athletes were
enlisting for service in the armed
forces. James Ballentine enlisted with
his younger brother Fred in May 1917.
Fred was a "brilliant quarterback"
according to the Minneapolis Tribune
and was set to be captain of the
Central High School football team for
the 1917 season. Around the country,
teams were so depleted that the 1917
college football season was nearly
canceled. Before the season could
start, both James and Fred were
off to training.

- - -

CHAPTER 2: Soldier

- - -

James Ballentine enlisted in the
US Army in May of 1917, just a few
weeks after the United States had
declared war on Germany. He was
ordered to report to Fort Snelling
for duty shortly after. He was ini-
tially denied entry after the doc-
tors concluded that he would not be
able to march or walk any distance
based on the condition of his feet.
The decision was quickly reversed
after Ballentine returned with documents showing his track records
including the State indoor record
for the quarter-mile which he ran
in just over 52 seconds in 1912.

By the time of Ballentine's enlistment, the Great War was already in its third year. The war started in the summer of 1914 with the assasination in Sarajevo of Archduke Franz Ferdinand, the heir-apparent to the throne of the Austro-Hungarian Empire. The United States remained isolationist, fatigued from recent foreign entanglements and unwilling to engage in another conflict on the other side of an ocean. During this time, the US was clearly sympathetic to the countries opposing Germany and the Austro-Hungarian Empire. The Americans were steadily supplying the Allies with money, raw materials, food, horses and munitions.

In September of 1917, James Ballentine boarded the USS Manchuria in Hoboken, New Jersey, with about 5,000 other soldiers bound for France.

Ballentine arrived in France unat-
tached to a specific unit and was sent
to machine gun school near the city
of Nancy, or possibly at the larg-
er training facility closer to Verdun
where up to four divisions were being
trained.

USS Manchuria in 1919 with soldiers bound for home.
Ballentine was not among them.

Most of the battles in 1917 had been
taking place farther north along the
Western Front, including the Third

Battle of Ypres in Belgium in July-November 1917. The American positions were farther south, and American activity on the front lines was very limited until October 1917.

As the American troop presence was building, the numbers of soldiers arriving each day would exceed 10,000. By May 1918, the American troops along the Western Front would surpass one million. By war's end in November 1918, that number would be more than two million.

German commanders anxiously observed this growing American presence. They moved with urgency to break through the Allied lines to inflict maximum casualties, and potentially capture Paris before the Americans could get established. Germany came very close to succeeding, but for a key battle,

and the first significant contribution
of the American forces. Over three
weeks in June 1918, 60 miles east of
Paris at the Battle of Belleau Wood,
the Americans would sustain over ten
thousand casualties but shut down the
German forces that had broken through
the Allied lines. The Americans then
proceeded to lead a series of attacks and counter attacks until, on
June 26, a message was sent: "Woods
now U.S. Marine Corps entirely." The
Americans were revered as heroes.

The next week was July 4th, 1918. In
Paris, the celebrations for American
Independence Day surely rivaled any-
thing in America itself. The French
crowds packed the streets of the
Place de la Concorde, within sight
of the Eiffel Tower, to see the
American forces marching in formation.

American soldiers parading through Paris
for Independence Day, July 4th, 1918

The war was far from over, but after
four years of stalemates and mass casualties along the Western Front with
little to show for it, there was now
reason for optimism. The recently arrived Americans were fresh, young and
strong, and their uniforms were new
and clean. The sheer numbers of them
brought much-needed hope to the city
that had just come terrifyingly close
to invasion. Most of the Americans
had not yet seen battle, let alone a

mass of cheering crowds in what certainly appeared as a magical city to
many of them.

Later that day in Paris, James
Ballentine suited up in a differ-
ent, but very familiar, uniform as he
prepared for a track competition in a
stadium filled with 20,000 spectators.
A field of former college athletes had
been assembled for the day. Despite
being out of competition for several
months, James pulled away from the
field winning the 100-yard dash with
a time just over 10 seconds. He then
proceeded to win the 200-yard dash in
a hair over 24 seconds, and captured
a third victory as part of the mile
relay. The news of his triumphs at
the event was slow to get across the
pond. It was not until after James'
letter to his brother John arrived,
that the press picked up on the

story of the meet. On August 11th,
James was on the front page of the
sporting section of the Minneapolis
Sunday Tribune.

- - -

Minnesota Boys Star
in Paris Track Meet

Jimmy Ballentine and Roy
Klein Take Honors in
July 4 Festival.

CHAPTER 3: Hero

- - -

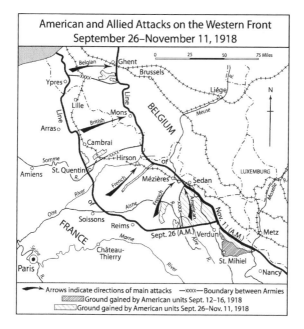

American and Allied Attacks on the Western Front
September 26–November 11, 1918

Ballentine in the 3d Division, 30th Infantry,
active between Verdun and Sedan

Five weeks later along the Western
Front, the American, French, British,
and Belgian troops would launch the
final decisive offensive of the Great
War with a rapid succession of attacks
along the entire length of the
Western Front.

Beginning on September 26, 1918, the
Americans and French armies pushed
north toward Sedan, France while the
British and Belgians attacked east-
ward toward Ghent, Belgium. These
battles would consume tens of thou-
sands more lives in just a matter
of weeks, but they would result in
the final armistice that was signed
on November 11th.

James Ballentine was moved toward
the front lines starting on September
28, 1918, when he arrived at Bois
de Hess, just south of Montfaucon.

This land of rolling farm fields and
forests a few years earlier had become a ghastly wasteland of shell
craters filled with mud, barbed wire
remnants, broken trees, trenches,
and uniforms left unclaimed after the
retrieval of the dead. Troops slept
in tents or rolled up in their coats.
The threat of nighttime mustard gas
attacks lead some men to sleep with
their gas masks on.

On October 2nd or 3rd, Ballentine's
unit proceeded northward into
Montfaucon. The town had been
completely destroyed before his
arrival. No buildings were standing
and the large church was reduced to
a set of columns and a few sections
of walls with arches.

Montfaucon. Photo from National Archives taken
October 2, 1918, within a day of Ballentine's arrival.

Today, where the town once stood,
there is an American monument standing 200 feet above the remains of
the church with a panoramic view of
the surrounding patchwork of fields
and forest. After the war the town
was rebuilt a couple hundred meters
down the road.

On the night of October 6-7,
Ballentine and his unit moved to
relieve positions at the front. They
held their position there until

they received orders on the night of
October 8-9 that they would attack
at 9:00a on the 9th.

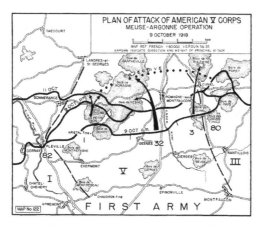

Plan of Attack for October 9, 1918

Their orders were to proceed from
their jumping off point on the
southern slopes of Hill 253, moving
northward across an open valley,
capture the hill called Bois de
Cunel, and then take the town
of Cunel.

Selected excerpts from the book:
3d Division Summary of Operations in
the World War

> *"The hour of attack was announced as*
> *8:30 a.m., October 9, following a*
> *19 1/2-hour artillery preparation.*
> *The 3d Division was assigned the*
> *mission of cleaning up the*
> *Bois de Cunel ..."*
> *"A smoke screen was to be placed on*
> *the southern edge of Bois de Cunel*
> *at 8:20 a.m. ... to cover the*
> *advance of the 30th infantry."*

Overnight, a cold rain was falling,
turning the ground to mud and fill-
ing the shell holes with water. The
troops lay there, on the side of Hill
253 across a small valley from their
first objective, Bois de Cunel. Orders
were received at 2:45a to delay the
attack until 9:12a.

As morning arrived, there was a misty
fog hanging over the valley. The
smoke screen was laid down. It mixed
with the fog and concealed the initial attack. Ballentine and his men
charged into the valley toward the
Bois de Cunel.

> *"On the right, the 3d Battalion, 30th*
> *Infantry, with the 2nd Battalion in*
> *support, moved through a heavy mist*
> *and a smoke screen to the southern*
> *edge of Bois de Cunel. About 10 a.m.,*
> *it entered the wood and received fire*
> *from Ferme de la Madeleine.*
> *Elements of Companies K and L engaged*
> *in a firefight with troops at the farm.*
> *Later, Companies E and F, of the*
> *leading wave succeeded in capturing*
> *the farm. ... By noon the attack*
> *had reached the northern edge of*
> *Bois de Cunel, where a line*
> *was consolidated."*

Lieutenant James Ballentine went into
his first battle with Lieutenant H.A.
Ambler on the left, and Lieutenant
Horace Smith on the right. They made
their objective, taking the top of
the Bois de Cunel within a couple
of hours.

Enemy shells arrived from the top of
the Bois and machine gun fire came
from Madeleine Farm across the road
to the right.

Madeleine Farm in 1918.
Bois de Cunel is on the left.

Around noon, just after taking Bois
de Cunel, Ballentine and Ambler were
still under heavy fire with shells
whistling overhead and landing nearby. They were jumping into and out
of craters created by the previous
rounds. One shell landed close and
Ambler was hit in the leg by some of
the shrapnel. Ballentine assisted him
with a first-aid bandage, then Ambler
told him to move ahead while he went
to a dressing station at the rear.

In the moments after leaving Ambler,
on his way to rejoin his platoon,
James Ballentine was killed. It was
October 9th, 1918, just after noon.

The details of his death, like so
many others, are lost to the memory
of the land. It is only from the first
hand accounts of Ambler and Smith
that we have the picture we do.

From their letters we know that
Ballentine had the compassion and
steadiness under fire to help his
fellow soldier, and he had the
bravery to press forward to rejoin
the attacking line.

- - -

Through our imagination, one can see
his final steps. A haze of smoke.
The whirring zip of bullets from enemy machine gun positions at the farm
to his right. Shells exploding the
land upward in arcs of wet dirt.
Ballentine leaving Smith, rising up
and pressing ahead to return to the
front line. Up and over the edges of
the shell craters with his rifle in
one hand and securing his helmet
with the other as he covered himself
at the sound of an incoming shell.
Rising again and again. Each time
he would rise up and move forward.

He sees Ambler's men ahead. He thinks
it is about forty yards and a memory flashes through him -- the drag of
the finish line tape across his chest
-- and he nods his head and smiles at
the odd ways these thoughts arrive.
"If the ground were flat, I could make
it in just under five seconds. This is
probably eight seconds, no more than
ten."

James Ballentine gritted his teeth
and steadied his eyes. He climbed up
and rose into a full sprint. The
enemy gunners, unable to adjust for
his speed, missed him repeatedly.

Behind the enemy line a soldier
leaned over and brought the next
shell into position. The explosion
jolted the gun back into its wooden
braces. The shell let out a scream
as it tore through the air above

the advancing Americans of the 30th
Infantry. James Ballentine was in
a full sprint to the finish as the
ground split open in front of him.
The force pulled him off the ground.
His back arched and his arms opened.
He felt the tape dragging across
chest as he gently slowed his burning
legs. A single word floated into his
mind, as it had so many times before.

Victory.

- - -

Photos of Madeleine Farm, 2019

Bois de Cunel is on the left.

Madeleine Farm from base of Bois de Cunel.

CHAPTER 4: Armistice, Waiting

- - -

On November 11, 1918, word of the
Armistice spread quickly around the
globe. It triggered spontaneous
celebrations in all the major capi-
tals of Europe and America, where
the news arrived instantly via
trans-Atlantic telegraph cables.

In Minneapolis, the news arrived just
after two o'clock in the morning, and
within a couple of hours, the streets
of downtown were filled with people
celebrating the end of the war. The
"boys" and women from "over there"
would be coming home soon. Later in
the morning, Minneapolis Mayor Thomas

Van Lear, declared the day an offi-
cial holiday and requested that all
businesses close at 2:00 pm to allow
workers to participate in the celebrations.

Celebrations in Minneapolis on November 11, 1918

For most of the families and friends
of soldiers around the world, their
celebrations were sincere but incom-
plete. There was no immediate news
regarding their sons, brothers, and
fathers -- and their daughters, sis-
ters, and mothers -- only that the

guns had gone silent. If their loved
ones were alive, or perhaps injured
but recovering, there was no way for
them to know. They only knew that
they were now free of further harm
at the hands of men.

After November 11th, their lives
undoubtedly returned to a daily rou-
tine perforated with anxious moments
waiting for some news -- news that
they wanted and also feared. Letters
from the front had arrived only on
the rarest of days, and newspapers
had provided scant hints of where
specific troops were, whether they
were engaged in battles, suffering
from influenza, or resting safely behind the lines. Now that the war was
over, it was all about the waiting.

This was undoubtedly true for the
family of Stuart and Helen

Ballentine of Minneapolis. Their
sons James and Fred had both enlisted in May of 1917, just a few weeks
after the US had declared war on the
Central Powers. They were both de-
ployed to France, with James going
first to machine gunner training, and
Fred arriving after doing a tour of
duty at the Mexico border. Fred remained in France until his return in
May of 1919. They had no information
on James other than some vague information that he was injured.

It was not until March 1, 1919, that
a telegram addressed to Helen
Ballentine arrived, simply stating:

> *"Deeply regret to inform you that it
> is officially reported that Lieutenant
> James J. Ballentine infantry died
> date and cause to be determined.*
>
> *Harris*
> *The Adjutant General 3PM"*

It is nearly unimaginable to picture
the Ballentine family living four
months since the end of the war, and
almost five months after James' death
in the Argonne, before receiving the
tragic news. Not until later in the
summer would more details emerge.

On March 18, 1919, before heading
to Washington where he would be on
the Foreign Affairs Committee, new-
ly elected Rep. Walter H. Newton
traveled to France to visit various
battleground sites where soldiers
from Minnesota had been active. Some
of the troops were still stationed
there, and we can assume Rep. Newton
was making inquiries regarding the
deaths of soldiers from his district
including James Ballentine. It was
only a couple weeks prior to Newton's
trip that the Ballentine family received the telegram confirming James'

death. It is conceivable that James'
father, Stuart, was in contact with
Rep. Newton in advance of his trip
to France. This may be part of the
reason Rep. Newton had gathered what
appeared to be a great level of detail regarding James. In a letter to
Stuart, Rep. Newton stated that James
was buried at Madeleine Farm while
he was there, which indicates that
James had been in another temporary
grave from the time of his death until Newton's trip in March 1919. We
know that James was soon after moved
to the American Cemetery at Romagne
where he remained until 1921, when
his body was disinterred and returned
home for burial with full military
rites at Lakewood Cemetery in
Minneapolis.

After his return, Rep. Newton received responses from two of

Ballentine's fellow officers, Lieutenant Horace Smith and Lieutenant H.A. Ambler. Their letters, when combined with the military records of the operations on October 9, 1918, provide us with a view into the final moments of Lieutenant James Jerome Ballentine, the son, athlete, and officer from Minneapolis who made the ultimate sacrifice for his country.

- - -

CHAPTER 5: Letters

- - -

Letter from fellow officer, Horace Smith, to US Rep. Walter Newton

May 4th, 1919

Mr. Walter H. Newton
Dear Sir:

Captain Powell turned your let-ter over to me to answer. In a way I feel guilty of having neglected late Lt. Ballentine's parents. It is much easier to write to you. First I will give you facts as I knew them and then try to excuse my negligence.

We had moved up to Bois de Hess

as Corps Reserve. Lt. Ballentine
joined us there about the twen-
ty-eight of September. Moved to Bois
de Montfaucon in support, about the
second or third of October. Relieved
the front positions on night of 6-7.
Lt. Ballentine was with our first Platoon about two o'clock, Lt. Ambler
was in command. It was nasty business
and twenty-four hours work a day. We
attacked on October 9th. Lt. Ambler
and Lt. Ballentine with first platoon
on the left. They made the objective
(Bois de Cunel). I picked up platoon about two hours after with no
officers, my own platoon was out of
action.

The men said Lt. Ambler had been
wounded through the leg and they saw
Lt. Ballentine giving some kind of
assistance and said they thought he
had been wounded slightly and was
waiting for first aid.

There was of course the usual

*artillery turned on the lately cap-
tured ground. Lt. Ballentine's section had lost heavily and there was
not a man that could give any sat-
isfactory information. I have every
reason to believe that on his way to
platoon after having helped Ambler he
was killed. Capt. Ambler is now at
Ward 26 A. U.S. Gen. Hosp. #28 Ft.
Sheridan, Ill. Write to Capt. Ambler
mentioning my name, please.*

*You can see what circumstances we
were in. We did not know anything
about Lt. Ballentine personally. He
was well liked by all of us in the
short time we had been to-gether.
Your letter is the first I knew of his
death for a certainty. One cannot
write letters without information.
Lt. Homan was wounded the same day
and knows nothing about that section
of the line.*

*Could you tell me if Lt.
Ballentine was wearing a ring.*

Hope this will give you what
is wanted.

> *Very truly yours.*
> *Horace B. Smith*
> *1st Lt. 30th Infy.*

Letter from fellow officer, H.A. Ambler, to US Rep Walter Newton

St. Louis, Mo.
June 7, 1919

Mr. Walter H. Newton
Washington, D.C.

Dear Sir:

Regret very much that the information I can give in regard to Lt. Ballentine must be indefinite as Lt. Smith stated. Lt. Ballentine was assigned to my platoon and given charge of one of the sections. After going into the line on October 7th, I saw

very little of him until the morning
of the 9th for the guns were at some
distance from each other and it was
necessary for him to remain with his
section. About midnight of October
8-9 orders were received that we
would attack at 9 O'clock the 9th.
I immediately started to locate Lt.
Ballentine and on finding him, gave
him instructions for the time and
place of the attack.

We had a little trouble in get-
ting the men lined up for we had no
trenches and had to line up in a
patch of wood. Being under fire at
the time. As it was Lt. Ballentine's
first time in action, I told him to
stay pretty close to me so I could
help him out if necessary. During the
confusion of the attack I lost sight
of him for a while, but after we had
gone a half mile he came back.

About that time the Boche started
shelling intermittently, and we

were hitting the holes together as
we heard the shells whistle.

The third one was pretty close
and a scrap of it caught me in the
foot. Lt. Ballentine helped me with a
first aid bandage. I then told him to
go ahead with the platoon I got back
to a dressing station almost immediately and saw nothing further of the
Lieut.

I knew Lt. Ballentine better than
any of the other officers and can
assure you that he was an excellent
officer, altho [sic] he had never been
in action before he was unafraid of
anything the Germans had, and by his
cool actions did much to keep the men
under control when the fire was hot.

Certainly was sorry to hear of
his death and regret that I cannot
give you more definite information.
At any time, there are any questions
that I can answer will be more than
glad to do so.

Very Truly Yours.

Capt. H.A. Ambler.

Ward 26th.

Usgh #28.

Ft. Sheridan, Ill.

Letter from US Rep. Walter H. Newton to Stuart Ballentine (James' father), undated

Mr. S.A. Ballentine,
3613 Harriet Avenue,
Minneapolis Minnesota

My dear Mr. Ballentine:

This engagement was in the Argonne and involved an advance on the part of the Third Division from a point in and around Nantillois upon a village just north of there by the name of Cunel. The road from Nantillois ran almost due north and south, as I recall it. The Germans were strongly

entrenched in the woods in and around
the place called Madeleine Farm.
Jimmie's regiment advanced up through
this road and the surrounding terri-
tory and took Madeleine Farm.

A temporary cemetery was con-
structed. It was at this point that
Jimmie was buried when I was over
there. Immediately after I left all
of the bodies in this particular
cemetery were removed to the national
cemetery at Romagne.

                    With kind regards, I am
                        Yours sincerely,
                        Walter H. Newton

CHAPTER 6: Post 246

- - -

The Veterans of Foreign Wars James
Ballentine Post 246, was founded in
Minneapolis on November 9, 1919, two
days before the first anniversary of
the end of World War I. At that time
in Minneapolis, VFW Patterson Post 7,
which started in 1902, was seeing a
rapid increase in membership as veterans returned from their service in
Europe. Post 7 had become the largest
VFW post in the nation. In June 1919,
a small group of veterans living in
the Lake Street area joined together
in gathering enough members to form
a new VFW post closer to home. They
met at the Calhoun Commercial Club,

located in the Calhoun Building which
still stands today at 711 West Lake
Street near Lyndale. By October 1919,
the group had assembled a list of 50
charter members and officers. They
selected the name of the post to be
"Ballentine Post 246", and included
one Honorary Member, Stuart A.
Ballentine, the father of James J.
Ballentine.

For the first several decades, the
Post continued to hold meetings in
the Calhoun Building. In 1954, the
VFW built its own space just north
of Lake Street on Lyndale. The building at 2916 Lyndale Avenue South has
been the home of Post 246 for over
65 years, serving as center of support and community for veterans. Over
these several decades, the Members
of Post 246 has included veterans
from wars and overseas conflicts both

large and small, from all branches
of the United States armed services,
from the 1890s through the recent and
current overseas conflicts of today.
Current membership is around 500
veterans.

The Veterans of Foreign Wars is a
national organization, established
in 1899. As a veterans organization,
each post is governed by a specific section of the IRS code (section
501(c)(19)). It requires that any
such organization be operating for
one or more of the purposes listed,
which includes promoting general
social welfare of the community,
providing and promoting care for
needy and disabled veterans, providing social and recreational activi-
ties for its members, and "to carry
on programs to perpetuate the memory
of deceased veterans and members of

the United States Armed Forces and
comfort their survivors."

On the second Tuesday of every month,
the Post holds its regular monthly
meeting for members of the Post and
its Auxiliary chapter (which is com-
prised of relatives of veterans of
foreign wars "within two degrees of
consanguinity").

Per Winston Kettle, recent Commander
at Post 246:

In 2015, the Post invested over $1M
in a major renovation of its home
at 2916 Lyndale Avenue South. This
included the expansion from one to
three separate bar spaces and the
addition of a full kitchen and a
live music venue. The investment
has increased revenues which is
enabling the Post to better serve

its members and the community.

*Ballentine Post 246 is a vibrant,
diverse and thriving Post at a time
when many VFW's are struggling. Our
diversity is our strength and we
reach out to many Veterans and community members by providing a welcoming
place for all to come together.*

*As a non-profit the Post makes dona-
tions, grants and loans to many
other non-profits in and around the
Twin Cities. With a passion for
Veterans and the community, the Post
has supported Minnesota Veterans
Homes, the VA Medical Center,
multiple youth sports programs and
youth leadership programs. The Post
also strongly supports Veterans and
community members that are most in
need by not only donating cash, but
by providing resources and leadership*

in combating homelessness and assist-
ing with other unmet needs.

In 2019, the Post partnered with and
hosted Governor Walz and his staff
to introduce his initiative to end
Veterans Homelessness by 2020.
The Post also partnered with other
organizations to start the Service
Provider Network which brings together all the local, state and national
players to discuss actions and
current needs for the Veteran community. This network aims to remove
"silos and road blocks" and open
lines of communication between the
various providers so that they can
better serve our nation's Veterans.

The Post also partnered with and
has agreed to fund unmet Veteran
needs with the Minnesota Assistance
Council for Veterans (MAC-V).

*This partnership will provide needed
funding to MAC-V and will allow the
Post to properly provide case management via professional social workers
to those Veterans in the most need.
Instead of offering cash and sending
someone down the road, the Post rec-
ognizes the need to not only provide
funding but to also provide professional help and case management for
the long term with housing, work,
transportation and other benefits the
individual may need.*

*The Post provides business advice and
mentoring to VFW's throughout the
nation on how to be a successful VFW.
The Post has hosted visitors from
several VFWs around the nation looking to see what we have accomplished
over the past few years.*

- - -

Exterior wall of Post 246 before renovation.

Current exterior wall of Post 246 with
flag mural by Scott LoBaido.

CHAPTER 7: Portrait

- - -

The Ballentine VFW is a unique place, a
unique space, with a unique personality.

On the wall you will find a portrait
of James Ballentine, and you will see
his stoic outline on the t-shirts
of the staff.

With a visit to the Ballentine VFW,
everyone sees the face of James. With
this small book, we hope a few more
people will see some of what is behind
the portrait.

— Nick & Craig

EPILOGUE: Backstory

- - -

This book was conceived by Nicholas and Craig across
a number of Thursday nights spanning multiple years
at the VFW Post 246. We were passionate about expe-
riencing and participating in the randomness of the
crowd, cheering for the bravest karaoke singers. The
VFW, we said, was "always on the way home" -- if we
stopped there, regardless of what direction we'd come
from, it was on the way home.

Our fluid minds began thinking about a book that
would contain some of the stories about the place (or
maybe a treasure map or guide to interesting people
you might meet). In January of 2016, Nick entered the
title "History of the Minneapolis VFW" into the annual
draft night for our local (only) chapter of the Manly
Book Club (MBC) where the eleven books for the year
are "pitched" and the selected through voting. It failed
to get enough support and was not voted in. It was a
really sorry pitch, not just because it was clear that

the book was not yet written. Then in January 2017, we rigged the voting (just a bit) by placing all of our twelve stickers on that one title. The book came in 10th in the rankings. We were in! Now we just needed to write the thing. Uh-oh. Neither of us had written anything (other than some drifty musings about gravel cycling on a pseudo site called "Gravel News Network").

Suddenly, our late evenings in the back bar had purpose -- we were doing research. We were writing a book. I started carrying a small blue notebook which ended up with a "sketch" of Trish the bartender, various chapter ideas, and some scribbles based on "interviews" with various patrons. In reality, the book wasn't moving along at all, and that may be the point when we started to think that perhaps it should be a treasure map instead. From the beginning we pictured it being something to be sold in a plexiglass brochure holder next to the register, maybe with an orange "Nice Price" sticker like the LPs of the 70s. Maybe $2.99. We would do it for the Post.

Then in August, 2017, during a car drive across the state of Minnesota to Gary, South Dakota, for the "Day Across Minnesota" gravel cycling event, we called the Post. On speakerphone, we shared our intent to write something (still undefined) with Winston, who was the

Post Commander at that time and whose name was somewhere in the little blue book. We wanted to let him know we were writing something, though we really didn't know what it was, and that we'd like to interview him to learn more about the Post. His reply was immediate and filled with enthusiasm. He loved the idea. The Post would be celebrating its 100th anniversary on November 9, 2019, and a book would be a great addition(!). We said that was over two years away so it should be no problem (though it's now October 2019 as this page is being written, just a few weeks away from that date which was so far away).

Winston agreed to meet with us for an (actual) interview and then showed us downstairs to the basement where there were new shelves with plastic tubs filled with every sort of artifact from old photo albums of 1960s holiday parties, to bundles of registration cards dating back to the 1920s. In one bin we found a document with "History of the Ballentine Post 246" on its cover, with metal binding, holding about 40 typed, carbon-copy pages.

Our first reaction was, "it's already been written!?!" and then we sat down to read it together. The document, written in 1931 by the Post Historian, Lester E. Nelson, contained a lot of the information that would end up in this small book. The letters describing the death of James Ballentine were profoundly simple and vivid. Farther into the pages, we found a list of the charter members of the post from its inception date of November 9, 1919. On that list, I placed my finger and slid down to the middle of the page where I saw the name "DEMAS, STEVE." My chest went tight, my eyes swelled, and I froze for a minute. I turned to Craig and said, "this is my grandfather."

I'd known my grandfather ("Papou") had been in World War I -- I'd somehow been allowed to bring his Purple Heart to school in 3rd grade for a project. Having grown up in Chicago, I had moved to Minneapolis nearly twenty years earlier, and for most of those years I didn't know about any Minneapolis (or VFW) connection of my family. About 5 years ago I was placing an old photo of my grandfather with his WWI Army unit into a frame and I noticed the penciled information on the back -- "2957 Lyndale Avenue South Minneapolis" followed by the names of the men in the picture. This street number 2957 is still above an unused door at the restaurant "It's Greek to Me" which is in a large old brownstone building across the street from the current location of the Post. The original bar is still in the restaurant, and I imagine the photo studio was in one of the units upstairs. Many times I have sat at the bar and imagined my grandfather there having a glass of red wine, his hair darker and blacker than the white shock of hair he had when I knew him in my youth.

The purpose of the book quickly evolved from character sketches and maps into something more deeply personal. I began researching the war and these two veterans, Ballentine and Demas, in parallel. Along the way I also learned about the significant impacts being made by Post 246 in the lives of our local veterans. I spent many weekend afternoons at the Minnesota History Center and days chasing loose threads often too far. I sent many failed attempts to potential Ballentine relations, watched movies and video series about the war, and I read and re-read Lester Nelson's 1931 history.

In September of 2019, I was in Munich for a couple weeks for work. When Friday arrived, I rented a car, packed in my bicycle and small bag, and drove to west to France, arriving in Metz around midnight. In the morning, I had a quick breakfast and drove to Verdun where I saddled up and rode on pavement, gravel, and grass paths, northwest to the American monument at the original location of the town of Montfaucon (which was rebuilt down the road after being completely destroyed in the war). Only some remains of the original church are standing there, with the sun casting shadows of the broken spines of the old church

onto the trimmed grass below. When Ballentine passed
through Montfaucon at the beginning of October 1918,
he would have seen the fullness of the destruction
there. He would have seen soldiers both alive and dead
as he moved up the road to Nantillois.

I pedaled up that road, through Nantillois, and as I
crested a ridge I could see I was approaching Bois de
Cunel and Madeleine Farm. I pulled into the small
road just before the farm that leads to a small German
cemetery. I laid my bike down and sat leaning against
a large tree looking at the farm and the hill behind
it. It was quiet except for the breeze passing through
the leaves over my head and some birds across the
field behind the farm. I heard some voices from the
farm buildings. A couple of girls, maybe ten years old,
walked their horses out of the barn and started riding.
They were laughing and joking with each other, letting
go of the reins and holding out their arms as they rode.
Their joyful sounds echoed across the woods.

I thought about the day almost 101 years prior when
the American soldiers of the 3rd division received
orders to proceed northward from Hill 253 to Bois de
Cunel, a small hill still covered in woods just across
the road from the farm. The troops would be moving
north, from left to right, from my position under
the tree. They would be digging into the base of the

hill, jumping into shell craters directly in front of
the enemy machine gun positions. The shells would
be screaming overhead, and men yelling and waving
directions at each other, then dropping flat and pulling
their helmets over their heads and bracing for incoming mortar, repeatedly taking what could be their final
breath --- and then standing up with rifle in hand and
pressing forward to the top of Bois de Cunel.

What would the American soldiers of the 3rd division
have traded for a minute of this quiet piece of shade
under this tree? And what would this shade under the
tree be if they had not made the sacrifices they did?
They didn't hear the sounds of the birds and the
voices of the girls riding in the pasture, yet they
made it possible. For that, and to them, we should
all give thanks.

- - -

APPENDIX: Charter Members
of Post 246

- - -

Dr. Russell R. Helm	Jan. 10, 1928--Jan. 8, 1929
Oscar J. Stearns, Jr.	Jan. 8, 1929---Jan. , 1930
Henry J. Jacobson	Jan. , 1930---Nov. 6, 1930
Glenn H. Zwale	Nov. 6, 1930---Nov. , 1931

The charter of the Post contains the names of the following members:

ARMSTRONG, Fred	3816 Bryant Av. So.
BALLENTINE, Fred S.	3613 Harriet Av. So.
HON. Ballentine, Stuart A.	3613 Harriet Av. So.
BEDOR, Louis J.	3145 Grand Av. So.
BREDAHL, Ernest	3018 Lyndale Av. So.
EHRNKE, Elmer	3529 Dupont Av. So.
BUDDE, John o.	3512 Fifth Av. So.
BURDICK, Eldon G. Jr.	139 West 40th St.
CARLSON, A. M.	3417 Oakland Av.
GONE, Theodore U.	3116 First Av. So.
CROSBETT, N. H.	3829 Stevens Av.
DENAS, Steve	3006 Harriet Av.
DOWNS, Harvey C.	5649 Colfax Av. So.
ENQUIST, Fred	3215 Pillsbury Av.
FISHER, Bennie R.	1411 Vine place
FRAZIER, Howard F.	3838 Nicollet Av.
FROST, Raymond M.	3716 First Av. So.
HALE, Frank E.	3628 Nicollet Av.
HANNAH, Conrad H.	2105 Lyndale Av. So.
HANSON, Reuben N.	3087 Bryant Av. So.
HART, Frank Z.	3916 Fifteenth Av. So.

List of charter members of Post 246, from 1931
document by L. Nelson (page 1 of 2)

- 64 -

HOLMES, Russell G.   4351 First Av. So.
JACOBSON, Henry J.   2815 Aldrich Av. So.
JENSEN, Harold J.   3850 Grand Av. So.
JOHNSON, Arnold I.   208 Park Av., Iowa Falls, Ia.
JORDAN, Edw. J.   3480 First Av. So.
LYNG, Dr. John A.   5049 Aldrich Av. So.
MAPES, Sallen F.   909 West Franklin
MOSLTER, Howard   910 Sixth Av. So.
NELSON, Geo. W.   4138 Wentworth Av.
OLSON, Lawrence C.   2940 Garfield Av. So.
PATTERSON, Lawrence W.   816 West Lake Str.
PETERSON, Gus. L.   3832 Lyndale Av. So.
PFAFF, Geo. F.   2637 Harriet Av. So.
POWERS, Geo. L.   209 East Ninteenth Str.
REECE, Glen F.   4015 Stevens Av.
RYAN, J. B.   3604 Harriet Av. So.
RYAN, J. C.   4   East Fourteenth Str.
SCHMIDT, A. E.   258 Hennepin Av.
SCHUNNET, Rudolph   4421 First Av. So.
SKELLARD, Arthur C.   2925 Grand Av. So.
SHELLY, Bert M.   4816 Colfax Av. So.
SCHULZ, Kenneth D.   325 East Fourteenth Str.
SCHULZ, Wm. C.   325 East Fourteenth Str.
SIEFORD, E. A.   1565 Spruce Place
SWEET, Glen A.   2917 Pillsbury Av.
THOMSON, T. H.   5525 Garfield Av.
VIGNESS, Jos. J.   215 Harvard Str. S.E.
WAGNER, Jos. J.   4749 Bryant Av. So.
WELO, Alfred G.   5035 Harriet Av.

List of charter members of Post 246, from 1931
document by L. Nelson (page 2 of 2)

Photograph of Nick's grandfather, Steve Demas,
(front row, 2nd from right) 42nd Division,
151st Field Artillery, ca. 1921

SELECTED BIBLIOGRAPHY

- - -

-- "History of the Minneapolis VFW" by Post Historian Lester Nelson in 1931, as found in the archives of Post 246

-- Minneapolis Morning Tribune: various dates as accessed from Minnesota Historical Society, Digital Newspaper Hub

-- To Conquer Hell, The Meuse-Argonne, 1918 by Edward G. Lengel

-- 3d Division, Summary of Operations in the World War by American Monuments Commission

-- Hennepin County Yearbook Collection

-- Hamline University, Digital Collections

-- University of Minnesota Yearbooks

-- Minnesota Historical Society Photo Archive Collection

-- Internal Revenue Service Code, Section 501(c) (19)

-- National Archives, Records of the American Expeditionary Forces (World War I)

-- Interviews with Winston Kettle, past-Commander of Post 246

-- Library Staff at Gale Library at the Minnesota Historical Society

ACKNOWLEDGMENTS

- - -

There are many people that we want to thank for their
contributions to this book. We would not have found
this story without Steve who runs the karaoke at the
Post. His welcoming way that has brought so many
great and terribly wonderful moments to the stage.
(Side note: I cannot sing and admit it openly, so I
stick to backup vocals/dancing, sometimes without
invitation). Next, we owe thanks to Winston Kettle
who was Post Commander at the time we started this
project. He welcomed us and encouraged us to dig into
the documents where the story and my family connection emerged. Then there are the members of the
Manly Book Club, Minneapolis Chapter (there are no
other chapters) for looking the other way when Craig
and I were over-voting on our own book. The staff at
the Minnesota History Center's Gale Library were of
immense help (and patience!) in gathering the initial
set of documents and newspapers. The guy I met at
the American monument at Montfaucon who told me

about the bunker hidden in the woods of Bois de Cunel
which I proceeded to locate along with a small pile of
unused German 78mm shells. The several friends who
reviewed drafts and provided feedback without which
the final story structure would not have been possible
(Bronwyn, Deepak, Alison, Sarah, Valerie and others).

And, of course, our families who gave us space and
time to get lost in our thoughts.

- - -

Made in the USA
Middletown, DE
15 July 2022

69476425R00045